Piecefully Amish

Connie Kauffman

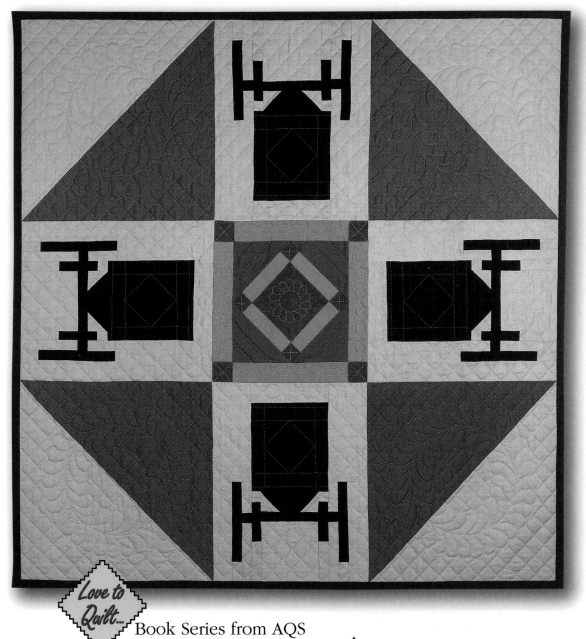

Love to Quilt... Book Series from AQS

American Quilter's Society
P. O. Box 3290 • Paducah, KY 42002-3290
www.AQSquilt.com

Located in Paducah, Kentucky, the American Quilter's Society (AQS) is dedicated to promoting the accomplishments of today's quilters. Through its publications and events, AQS strives to honor today's quiltmakers and their work and to inspire future creativity and innovation in quiltmaking.

EDITOR: SHELLEY HAWKINS
GRAPHIC DESIGN: TOM SULLIVAN
COVER DESIGN: MICHAEL BUCKINGHAM
QUILT PHOTOGRAPHY: CHARLES R. LYNCH
SCENIC PHOTOGRAPHY: BONNIE K. BROWNING

Library of Congress Cataloging-in-Publication Data
Kauffman, Connie.
      Piecefully Amish: AQS love to quilt series / by Connie Kauffman.
          p. cm.
      ISBN 1-57432-786-0
      1. Patchwork--Patterns. 2. Appliqué--Patterns. 3. Quilts, Amish.
I. Title.
TT835 .K382 2001
746.46'041--dc21   2001007574

Additional copies of this book may be ordered from the American Quilter's Society, PO Box 3290, Paducah, KY 42002-3290, or online at www.AQSquilt.com.

Copyright © 2002, Connie Kauffman

DEDICATION

This book is dedicated to my mother, Eileen Snyder, who taught me to sew and introduced me to the world of fabrics. She also taught me how to select colors and patterns that are pleasing to the eye and instilled in me a lifelong love of sewing.

ACKNOWLEDGMENTS

Thanks to my father, Wilbur Snyder, and my husband, Herman. Although they may not understand the process of sewing, they always appreciate the results.

My sisters, Karen and Margo, have shown through their own work that it's never too late to reach for your dream and make it a reality.

Special thanks to my sister, Jody, who helped brainstorm, motivate, and keep me going in countless ways. Her encouragement, enthusiasm, and sharing brought joy to the process of making this book possible.

Last but not least, thanks to my children, Andrew and Sara, who are my gentle critics and greatest givers of praise.

BEHIND A BUGGY

I am behind a buggy driving down a country road.
I start to take a look around while the car is moving slow –
I see the bright green pastures, the fields all tilled with care,
I feel the sun upon my face, the crispness in the air.

I am behind a buggy, it seems I'm at a crawl,
But this gives a chance to linger, and I do not mind at all.
The peaceful Amish lifestyle could teach us all so much,
If we could slow our "hurry," and give our souls a gentle touch.

I am behind a buggy, the horse continues on,
The rhythm of its canter makes an "earthy" song.
This unexpected gift of time amid a busy day,
Gives pause to see God's beauty, as I go on my way.

– Connie Kauffman

Contents

 When you see the black buggy, a helpful hint is nearby.

PREFACE

I consider myself lucky to live in a community that shares its roads with countless Amish buggies. There is striking beauty in their design and the horses that pull them. I have a great respect for the lifestyle of the Amish and steady pace of their lives. When slowing down while driving behind a buggy, I often wonder how it would feel to constantly travel at this speed. I think there are times it would do us all good to sit back and follow the gentle pace of a horse.

I truly hope you enjoy making the quilts in this book and that you will appreciate the simple beauty in every buggy you encounter.

Permission granted by those photographed.

A Bit of Buggy Background

In many present-day communities, horses and buggies share the roads with bikes, cars, and even semi-trucks. What a contrast in technology and lifestyle!

Today, buggies are like a piece of living history. Most of our ancestors rode in carts, wagons, and buggies before the invention of the automobile. The fact that several religious groups still drive buggies today is proof of the reliability, durability, and strength of their design.

Amish buggies vary a great deal from one community to another. The colors range from all black to buggies that have gray, yellow, white, rust, or brown tops. The basic shape and size of a buggy may also vary in subtle ways if you take time to look at the details. Buggies can have squared tops, curved tops and bottoms, or no covering at all. They may have no windows, one or two windows, or an oval window in the back. Some buggies have license plates while others do not. Rear-view mirrors are often located on one or both sides of a buggy. You may find other variations such as buggies with windshield wipers, etc.

To make buggy travel safer at night, many safety devices are now used by most communities, and some are required by law. Battery-powered lights appeared in the 1930s. Red taillights and blinking lights were added as extra safety precautions. Silver reflecting tape is another safety device, and it is used in quite a variety of patterns on the backs of buggies. It is interesting to see several buggies together and notice how the placement and design of these features vary from one buggy to another, even in the same community.

The orange triangle "slow-moving vehicle" sign is required for buggies in most areas, although the placement of this sign is not standard. You will see it located in different places on the back of buggies. The triangles also vary in color, ranging from orange to dark red, pink, or yellow. These safety features are a great help in identifying buggies on the road at night.

Look closely at the buggies you encounter and see in pictures. The colors and styles of the buggies, placement of lights, triangles, reflector tape, and mirrors are in countless variations. The differences you find may surprise and delight you.

The patterns with buggies in this book are simple images that illustrate the variety of buggies on the road today. All of the patterns show the back view of the buggies. If you travel or live in a community with many buggies, this is an interesting and familiar sight.

MAKING AMISH QUILTS

Quilters have admired traditional Amish quilts for many years. Early patterns, such as Sunshine and Shadow, Roman Stripe, Center Diamond, Four Patch, and Rail Fence, are part of the rich legacy of Amish quilting. Solid colors and beautiful, elaborate hand quilting are the hallmarks of these quilts.

If you want to make a traditional looking Amish-style quilt, viewing antique Amish quilts offers guidance on color, design, and style. These quilts can be found at shows, museums, a friend's house, or other displays. Nothing beats seeing the real thing. Books on Amish quilts are a great source for patterns and color combinations. If you find a quilt you are particularly drawn to, you may want to duplicate the colors in one of your own quilts.

Amish quilts were made using leftover solid-colored fabrics from clothing saved for quilting. Colors ranged from a deep, rich palette to ones with more muted-gray tones. Surprising color combinations often produced beautiful results.

Making a true Amish-style quilt is a matter of perspective. By using the patterns in this book, you can create a quilt that resembles an Amish quilt with patterns and colors you enjoy. If you really want to capture the essence of making an Amish-style quilt,

go to your fabric cupboard and remove all the solid fabrics. Your collection may be large or small; however, you may be surprised by how well the colors coordinate together. I did not have a lot of solid fabrics when I started this book, and black was a color I did not own. Now after making many Amish-style quilts, I love black fabric and the way it works with other colors.

Enjoy experimenting with new color combinations. It is fun to see how red pops out when surrounded by greens or blues. Add a touch of black to your palette. You can also trade fabrics with a friend to achieve a perfect combination. Choosing colors is one of the most exciting parts of quilt-making, so enjoy yourself!

Each traditional Amish pattern in this book is presented in two ways. The first quilt is made with solid fabrics and traditional quilting patterns. These solid fabrics showcase quilting nicely. The second quilt using the same pattern is designed with contemporary fabrics for a more modern look. Experiment with variations of color to enjoy the contrast the patterns present.

These traditional patterns are ageless in their simple design and beauty. I hope you enjoy working with these classic patterns that are still popular today.

GENERAL INSTRUCTIONS

BATTING

In choosing a batting, consider how you want your quilt to look. If you want the look of an old quilt, a thin batting should be used. Many antique quilts have cotton battings. For the quilts in this book, I used a thin poly-cotton blend. This is a nice batting for hand quilting. If a puffier look is preferred, a thicker polyester batting can be used.

QUILTING THREADS

Quilting on antique quilts was typically done in one color of thread, often white or black. This is a beautiful way to display quilting. However, we are richly blessed with a wide range of colors in quilting threads, so there are many options now. Before quilting, think of how you want to see the whole quilt. Do you want the quilting stitches visible, or do you want them to disappear into the background? Choosing a thread that matches the background fabric or a monofilament thread will make the quilting blend softly into the background of the quilt. Using a contrasting thread will draw more attention to the quilting stitches. When in doubt about what colors to quilt with, use one color throughout your quilt.

When quilting some of the buggies, I used a monofilament thread in the ditch around the buggies. A contrasting thread was used to accent the lines and designs in the buggies. The PEACOCK DIAMOND, page 52, was hand quilted in gold metallic thread. This gives an added sparkle to the quilt.

Experiment. Have fun stitching with new colors. Make a few quilts with only one color and see the contrast. Enjoy the best of the new and the old.

QUILTING DESIGNS

Amish quilts have a reputation for beautiful hand quilting and designs. Many of the early quilts had large patches which left open areas to fill with quilting. Some of the quilting designs include feathered borders and circles, single and double cables, cross hatching,

pumpkin seeds, and baskets. Solid fabrics provide a perfect background for these elaborate designs.

A variety of quilting patterns are provided in this book (page 55). The Amish-style quilts contain the more traditional patterns, while the variations of these quilts have contemporary quilting designs. Use these designs or select others to establish the look you desire for your quilt.

EMBELLISHMENTS

Embellishments are a fun way to add personality to your buggy quilts (Fig. 1). These final little details can make your buggy look more realistic.

Red and orange buttons are easy additions for taillights. Some buggies have two to six different lights visible from the back. Black or dark silver buttons can be used for rear-view mirrors. The buttons can be round or oval, whichever looks closest to the real thing.

Reflector tape is easy to duplicate by ironing adhesive backing on fabric, then cutting it into strips and fusing it to the buggy. You can use silver-colored fabric, although shades of gray look just as nice.

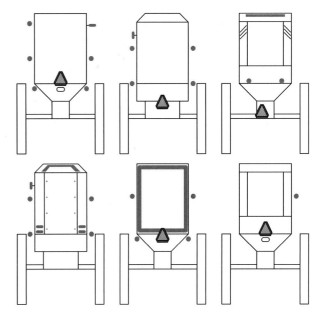

Fig. 1. Embellishment variations.

The orange triangle "slow-moving vehicle" signs may vary in color from yellow to orange, pink, and dark red. Triangles and license plates (Fig. 2) are simple shapes that are easy to copy and assemble with fusible interfacing. They look very close to what is seen when viewing a buggy from a distance. Be creative and explore different fabrics and colors.

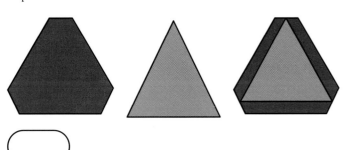

Fig. 2. Full-sized triangle and license plate patterns.

BINDING

All the bindings in this book are straight with over-lapped corners. Most antique Amish quilts use this method of binding, perhaps because it conserves fabric, because it was the traditional method, or just because it was easier than making mitered corners. This method of binding is easy and suits the patterns well. It is a good idea to *cut the binding strips first* to make sure you have the length of fabric needed before cutting out other pattern pieces. Always cut the binding a bit longer than required to allow for slight variations in the finished quilt size.

Summer buggy from Montgomery, Indiana.

Attaching the Binding

Square up the quilt and attach the binding as follows:

- Sew a binding strip to the front left and right sides of the quilt. Fold the binding to the back, turn under ¼", and hand stitch in place. Trim the ends of the binding even with the sides of the quilt.

- Sew the last two binding strips to the top and bottom edges of the quilt. Trim the ends of the binding to about ¼" beyond the quilt edge. Fold the ends to the inside, even with the sides, then fold the bindings over as previously described and hand stitch in place.

Casings

If you want to hang your quilt, sew a casing or hanging sleeve on the back. Cut a strip of fabric 8½" wide (4½" for wall quilts and miniatures) by the width of your quilt. Finish each end by turning the fabric under ¼" and stitching. Then, fold the strip in half lengthwise, right side out. Sew the raw edges together along the length of the strip to make a tube. Refold the casing tube so that the seam falls at the middle of the back of the tube, out of sight. Use a hand blind stitch to sew the top and bottom edges of the tube to the top back of the quilt (Fig. 3). The quilt is now ready to hang.

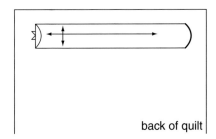

back of quilt

Fig. 3. Add a casing for hanging your quilt.

Labeling

It is important to label every quilt. A lot of time and creativity go into your quilts, so give yourself credit. Make your own labels or simply sign the back of the quilt. Be sure to attach your label before hanging the quilt. This will save you the hassle of taking the quilt down and will ensure you don't forget the label.

 I have found fabric-backed paper for the computer to be a quick and easy way to make quilt labels. Give it a try!

You can add as much information on a label as you want. Remember, this may be the only documentation your quilt has, so consider what you want to include. The following are some ideas of items to include on the label:

- The date you finished the quilt or the date you gave it as a gift. You may want to record the days, months, or years it took to make the quilt. Some quilts, just like children, take a long time to be born!

- The name of the person who did the piecing or quilting, if not yourself.

- Special occasion for making the quilt, such as wedding or birthday.

- Any special information, such as what batting was used. This can help future owners determine the best method of washing the quilt.

- The name of the quilt or the quilt pattern.

- Your signature.

BUGGY QUILTS
SHOOFLY DIAMOND

42" x 42"

The Center Diamond pattern in the middle block of this quilt is traditional and easy to make. The dark triangles and the Center Diamond square form the Shoofly pattern. A nice area for display of quilting designs is in the large corner blocks.

CHOOSING FABRICS

This quilt is made from solid fabrics, which is typical of Amish quilts. If you plan to make several buggy quilts, you may want to buy all the black fabric at the same time. Black can be a difficult color to match on a second trip.

FABRIC REQUIREMENTS

For those patches that can be rotary cut, dimensions are given with the patterns.

 Cut the large purple triangles before cutting the smaller pieces.

Fabric	Yards	Cutting Guide
Red	¼	1 N, 4 O, 4 S
Green	⅛	4 P, 4 R
Dark purple	¾	4 Q
corner blocks		2 squares 15 ⅞", cut once diagonally
Light purple	1¼	8 A, 4 B, 4 D, 8 E, 8 G, 8 H, 8 I, 8 J, 8 K, 8 L
corner blocks		2 squares 15⅞", cut once diagonally
Black	¾	4 C, 8 F, 8 I, 4 J, 8 K, 4 M
binding	4 strips 2" x width of fabric	
Backing	1⅓	
Batting	46" x 46"	

BLOCK CONSTRUCTION

This quilt has three main blocks. To simplify construction, the directions are given for you to create one block at a time.

Corner Blocks

Block trim size: 15½". Using the large purple triangles, lay one light purple triangle on top of one dark purple triangle. Sew along the long edge (Fig. 4). Open the triangle and press the seam to the dark fabric. Make four half-square units to form the corner blocks.

Fig. 4. Corner block assembly.

Buggy Blocks

Block trim size: 12½" x 15½". Refer to the buggy block assembly diagram, page 14, and make four buggy blocks. It is helpful to lay out your pattern pieces as shown in the diagram before sewing.

 Chain sewing the pieces makes constructing this block faster.

Center Diamond Block

Block trim size: 12½". Refer to the block assembly diagram, page 14, to make the Center Diamond block.

ASSEMBLING THE QUILT TOP

Lay out the nine blocks and sew them into three strips. Sew the strips together as shown in the diagram on page 14.

FINISHING YOUR QUILT

Layer the backing, batting, and quilt top and baste together. Quilt as desired, or refer to the quilting design, page 14. A 3½" quilting design fits in the middle square, and an 11½" design fits in the corner squares. Trim the quilt and add binding. Sew a casing to the back and sign your quilt as a finishing touch.

 Quilter's masking tape is a handy tool for making straight grid lines.

Diagrams for SHOOFLY DIAMOND

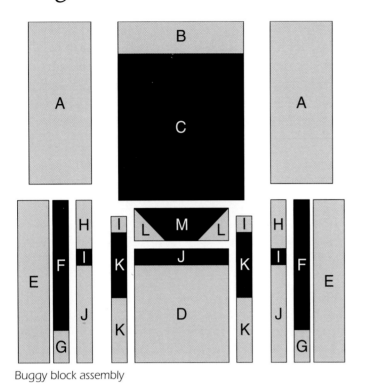

Buggy block assembly

Center Diamond block assembly

Quilting patterns on pages 55–61

11½" Feathered Circle, Quilting Stencil #141,
EZ Mark Stencils • Purdy, MO

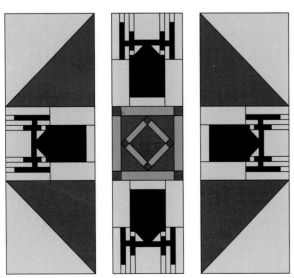

Quilt top assembly

Quilting design

Patterns for SHOOFLY DIAMOND

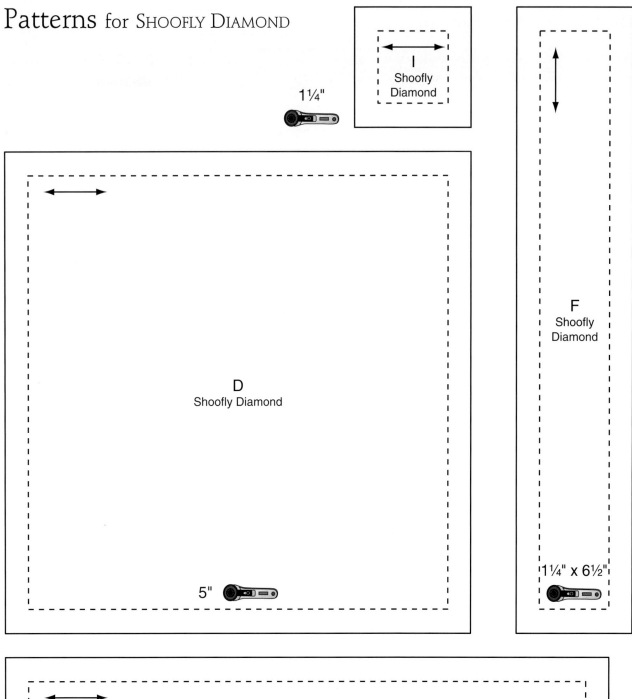

I
Shoofly
Diamond

1¼"

D
Shoofly Diamond

5"

F
Shoofly
Diamond

1¼" x 6½"

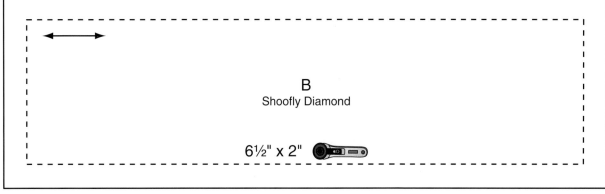

B
Shoofly Diamond

6½" x 2"

Patterns for SHOOFLY DIAMOND

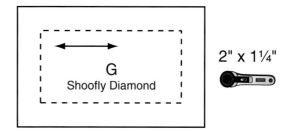

G
Shoofly Diamond

2" x 1¼"

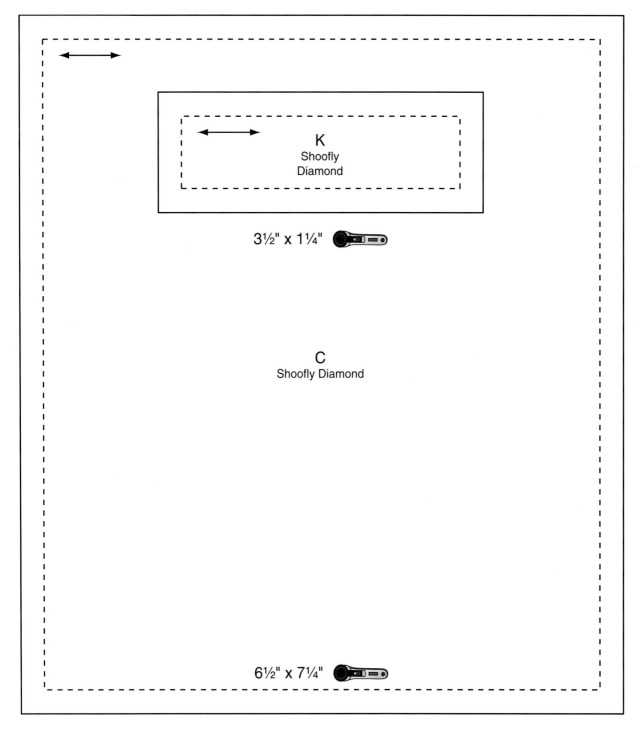

K
Shoofly
Diamond

3½" x 1¼"

C
Shoofly Diamond

6½" x 7¼"

Patterns for SHOOFLY DIAMOND

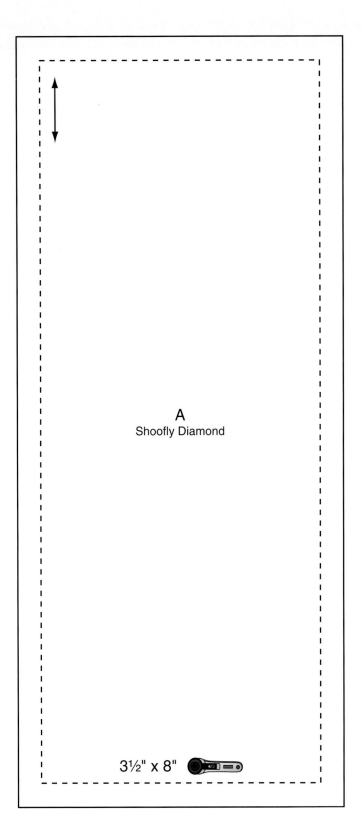

A
Shoofly Diamond

3½" x 8"

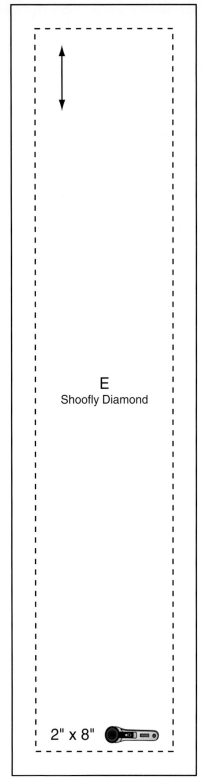

E
Shoofly Diamond

2" x 8"

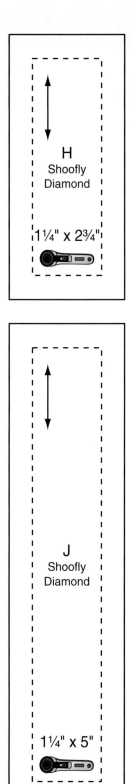

H
Shoofly
Diamond

1¼" x 2¾"

J
Shoofly
Diamond

1¼" x 5"

Patterns for SHOOFLY DIAMOND

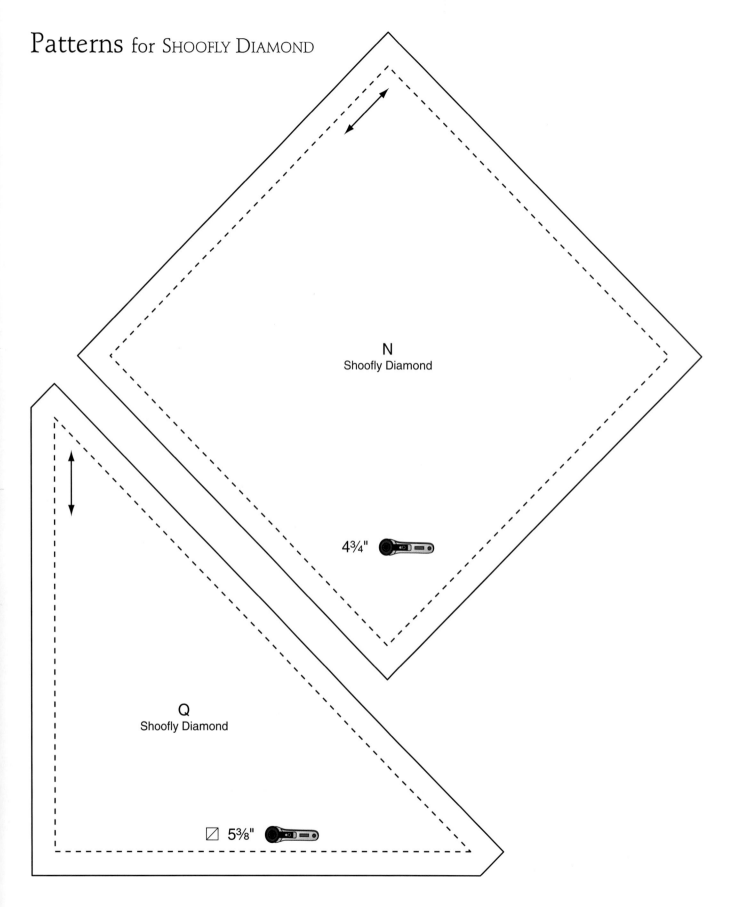

N
Shoofly Diamond

4¾"

Q
Shoofly Diamond

◻ 5⅜"

Patterns for SHOOFLY DIAMOND

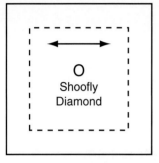

O
Shoofly
Diamond

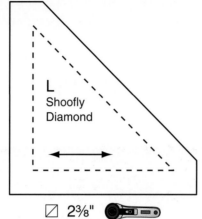

L
Shoofly
Diamond

◻ 2⅜"

S
Shoofly Diamond

2"

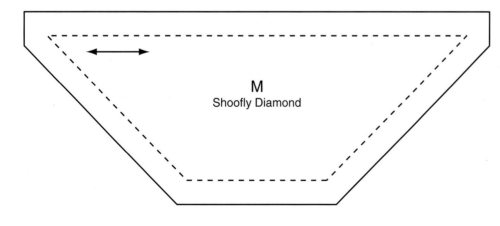

M
Shoofly Diamond

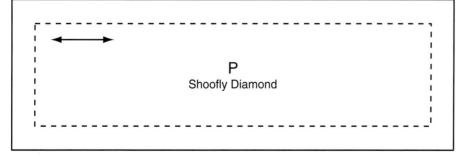

P
Shoofly Diamond

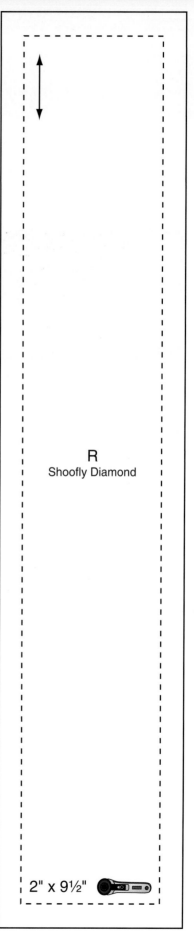

R
Shoofly Diamond

2" x 9½"

Bunches of Buggies

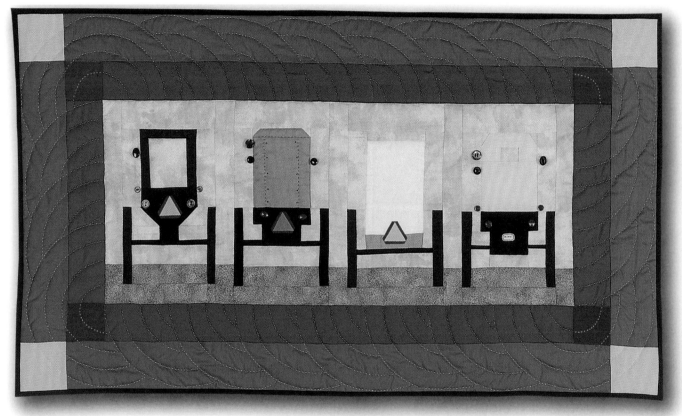

34" x 19½"

This quilt depicts four different styles of buggies representing various areas around the country. Each one is unique in its own way. These buggies lend themselves to a variety of embellishments.

CHOOSING FABRICS

The use of solid fabrics in the border gives the look of an older Amish quilt. Figured fabrics used to represent the sky and grass can make the buggy scene look more realistic. If your blue sky fabric has a directional print, cut eight E patches, page 25, on the horizontal grain and two on the vertical grain.

BLOCK ASSEMBLY

Block trim size (for each buggy block): 5½" x 11". Refer to the block diagrams, page 22, to make the Black, Gray, White, and Yellow Buggy blocks. It is helpful to lay out your pattern pieces as shown in the diagram before sewing.

This is one quilt for which you might like to use a variety of black fabrics to add dimension to the buggies. This is a good place to use scraps from different projects.

FABRIC REQUIREMENTS

For those patches that can be rotary cut, dimensions are given in the patterns. To keep track of the pieces, it's best to cut and make only one buggy at a time. A lowercase "r" indicates that a patch should be reversed.

Fabric	Yards
Red	⅛
Tan	⅛
Dark blue	⅜
Dark green	⅜
Sky blue	⅜
Grass green	⅛
Black	½
Gray	⅛
White	⅛
Brown	1¼" x 3½"
Yellow	⅛
Binding	3 strips 2" x width of fabric
Backing	¾
Batting	38" x 23½"

This quilt consists of four buggy blocks separated by sashing. Making each buggy block separately keeps the pieces you are working with at one time to a minimum.

Cutting Guide

Borders (cut and set aside)

Red	4 squares 2½"
Tan	4 squares 3"
Dark blue	2 strips 2½" x 11", 2 strips 2½" x 25½"
Dark green	2 strips 3" x 15", 2 strips 3" x 29½"

Sashing Strips

Sky blue	5 EE
Grass green	5 FF

Black Buggy Pieces

Sky blue	1 A, 3 E, 1 H, 1 Hr, 2 J, 1 AA
Black	2 B, 1 C, 1 D, 1 G, 1 I, 2 K, 2 L
Grass green	1 E, 1 F

Gray Buggy Pieces

Sky blue	3 E, 1 O, 1 Or, 2 P, 2 R, 1 AA
Black	1 D, 2 L, 1 Q, 2 S
Gray	1 M, 1 N
Grass green	1 E, 1 F

White Buggy Pieces

Sky blue	2 E, 1 C, 2 V, 1 X, 1 AA
Black	2 L, 1 W
White	1 M, 1 T
Brown	1 U
Grass green	1 E, 1 F

Yellow Buggy Pieces

Sky blue	2 E, 2 I, 2 P, 3 R, 1 AA, 1 BB, 1 BBr, 1 DD
Black	1 D, 2 L, 2 S, 1 Z
Yellow	2 R, 1 Y, 1 CC
Grass green	1 E, 1 F

Assembly Diagrams for BUNCHES OF BUGGIES

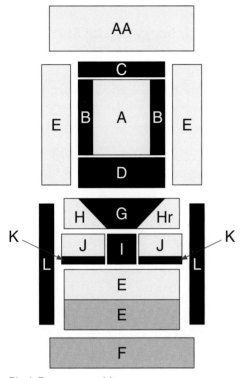

Black Buggy assembly

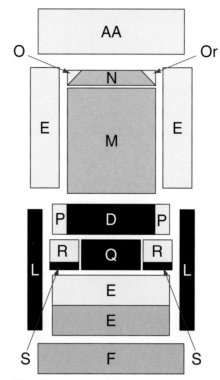

Gray Buggy assembly

EE

FF

Sashing

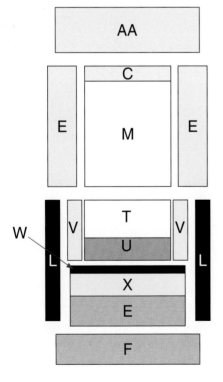

White Buggy assembly

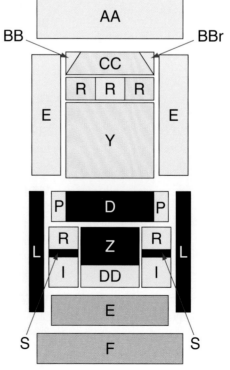

Yellow Buggy assembly

JOINING THE BLOCKS

Lay out the buggy blocks in the order you prefer and join them by sewing the sashing strip between each block as shown in the diagram. The sashing strip consists of a 1½" x 9" blue rectangle (EE) pieced with a 1½" x 2½" green rectangle (FF). Sew a sashing strip to each side of the row of buggies. The grass and sky should be in a horizontal line as you pin the pieces together. Square up the joined buggy blocks and sashing before adding the borders. Refer to the quilt top assembly diagram to add the borders to the buggy blocks.

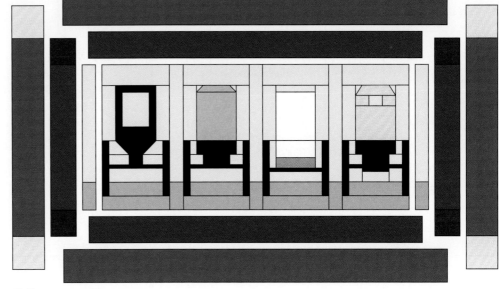

Quilt top assembly

FINISHING YOUR QUILT

Add any embellishments you like to the buggies. Buttons can be added after quilting. The snaps on the gray buggy can be made with small French knots.

Layer the backing, batting, and quilt top, and baste together. Quilt as desired, or refer to the quilting design. Notice how the fan design extends across both outside borders. This was commonly done on older Amish quilts. Trim the quilt and add binding. Sew a casing to the back and sign your quilt as a finishing touch.

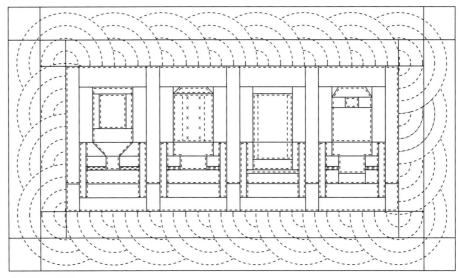

Quilting design

Quilting patterns on pages 55–61

Patterns for Bunches of Buggies

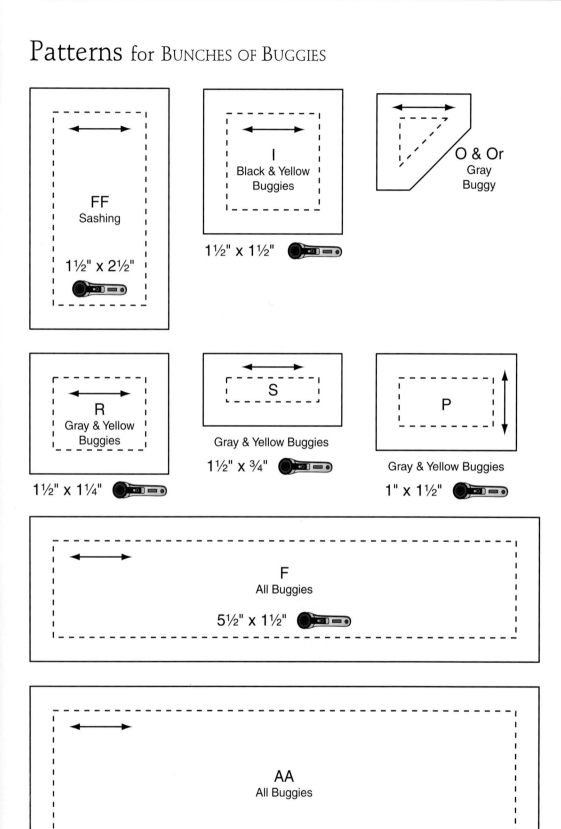

FF
Sashing

1½" x 2½"

I
Black & Yellow
Buggies

1½" x 1½"

O & Or
Gray
Buggy

R
Gray & Yellow
Buggies

1½" x 1¼"

S

Gray & Yellow Buggies

1½" x ¾"

P

Gray & Yellow Buggies

1" x 1½"

F
All Buggies

5½" x 1½"

AA
All Buggies

5½" x 2"

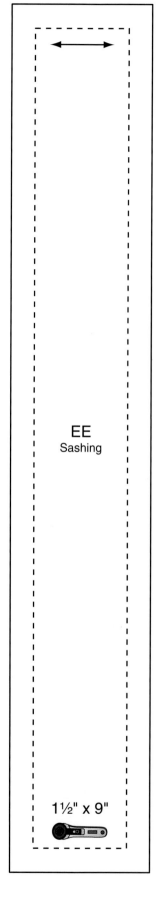

EE
Sashing

1½" x 9"

Patterns for BUNCHES OF BUGGIES

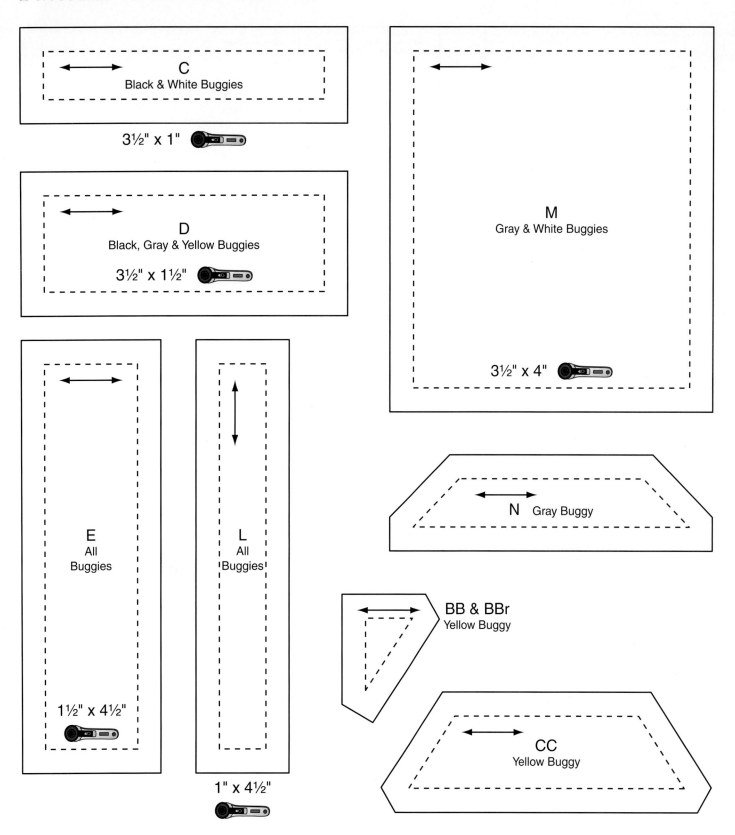

C
Black & White Buggies

3½" x 1"

D
Black, Gray & Yellow Buggies

3½" x 1½"

M
Gray & White Buggies

3½" x 4"

E
All
Buggies

1½" x 4½"

L
All
Buggies

1" x 4½"

N Gray Buggy

BB & BBr
Yellow Buggy

CC
Yellow Buggy

Patterns for BUNCHES OF BUGGIES

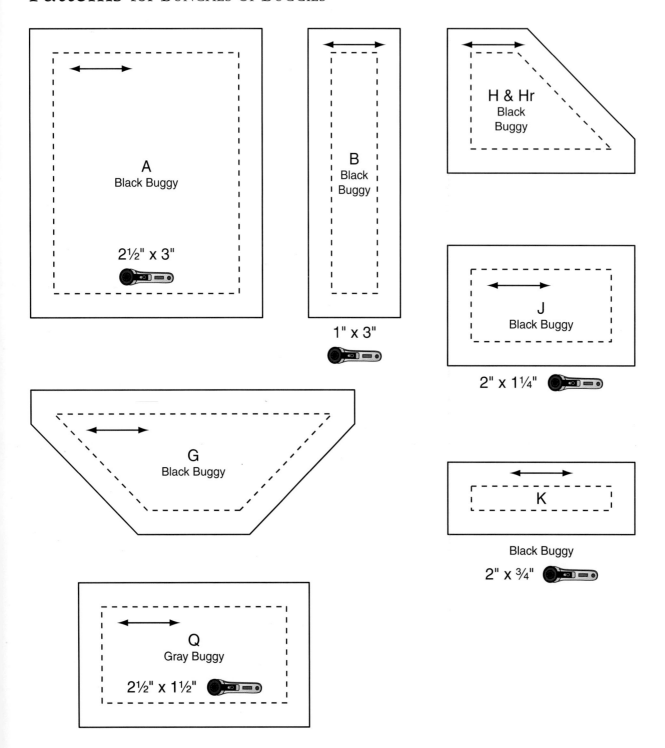

A
Black Buggy

2½" x 3"

B
Black Buggy

1" x 3"

H & Hr
Black Buggy

J
Black Buggy

2" x 1¼"

G
Black Buggy

K

Black Buggy

2" x ¾"

Q
Gray Buggy

2½" x 1½"

Patterns for BUNCHES OF BUGGIES

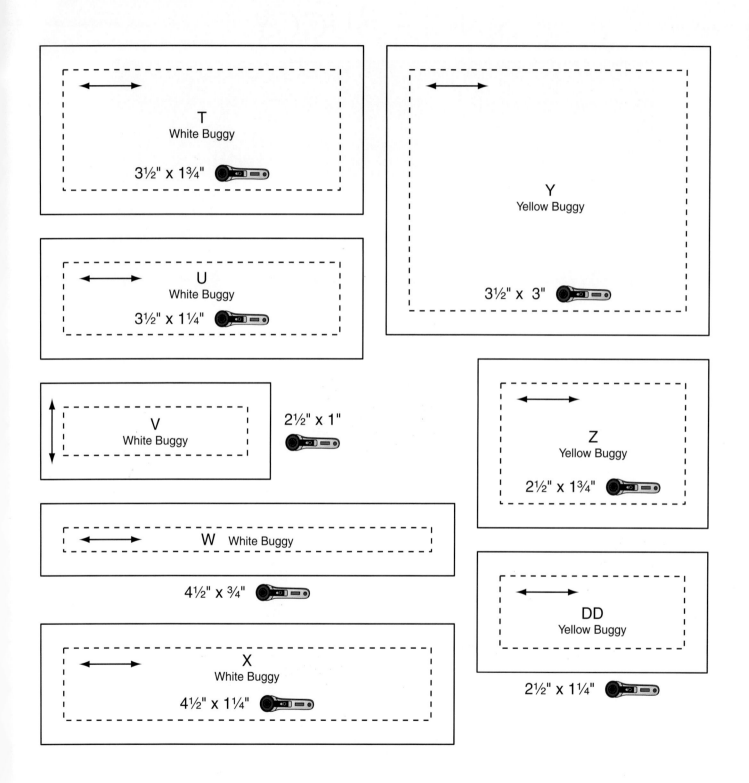

T
White Buggy

3½" x 1¾"

U
White Buggy

3½" x 1¼"

V
White Buggy

2½" x 1"

W   White Buggy

4½" x ¾"

X
White Buggy

4½" x 1¼"

Y
Yellow Buggy

3½" x 3"

Z
Yellow Buggy

2½" x 1¾"

DD
Yellow Buggy

2½" x 1¼"

SINGLE BUGGY

11" x 14"

When creating this quilt, you can choose any of the four buggy patterns from the quilt BUNCHES OF BUGGIES for the center block. Create the Flying Geese border using traditional piecing, or try the accuracy of foundation piecing.

CHOOSING FABRICS FOR BORDERS

Be creative in choosing the fabric for your Flying Geese border. Use solid-colored fabric if a more traditional Amish look is desired. Printed fabrics will still produce an Amish look as long as traditional Amish colors are used.

FABRIC REQUIREMENTS

BUGGY WITH BLUE AND FUCHSIA BORDER

For those patches that can be rotary cut, dimensions are given with the patterns.

Fabric	Yards	Cutting Guide
Blue	1/8	34 A
Fuchsia	1/4	68 B, 4 C
Purple	1/8	4 C
Binding		2 strips 1¼" x 13"
		2 strips 1¼" x 16"
Backing	1/2	
Batting		15" x 18"

BUGGY WITH BLACK BORDER, page 31

Black/white	1/8 total of various prints	34 A of different colors, 4 C of same color
Light gray print	1/4	68 B, 4 C
Black binding	1/8	2 strips 1¼" x 13" 2 strips 1¼" x 16"
Backing	1/2	
Batting		15" x 18"

BLOCK CONSTRUCTION

Block trim size: 7½" x 10½". Choose a buggy from those on page 20 for the center block. Add sashing strips (EE and FF units) to both sides of the block.

 All colors for the buggy block require less than 1/8 yard, except when foundation piecing the border. This is a good time to use small pieces left over from other projects. The fabric in the sky and grass blocks can be changed to complement the border if desired.

BORDER CONSTRUCTION

Refer to the assembly diagram, page 30, and sew two B patches to each side of an A patch. Make 34 units. Lay out the units as shown and sew two strips with 10 units and two strips with seven units.

If you prefer to foundation piece the border, refer to the foundation piecing guides on page 32. An additional 1/8 yard of each border fabric is required.

ASSEMBLING THE QUILT TOP

Refer to the quilt top assembly diagram, page 30, to join the blocks and borders. After sewing the two side borders, trim the buggy block to fit the Flying Geese units.

FINISHING YOUR QUILT

Add any embellishments you like to the buggy block. Buttons can be added after quilting.

Layer the backing, batting, and quilt top, and baste together. Quilt as desired, or refer to the quilting design, page 30. Trim the quilt and add binding. Sew a casing on the back and sign your quilt as a finishing touch.

When foundation piecing, leave the paper on the back until the binding is sewn. It is easier to sew the binding on before removing the paper. After the binding is sewn to the quilt, remove the paper, layer, and baste your quilt. After quilting, carefully trim the batting and backing only, and turn the binding over to the back to finish.

Diagrams for SINGLE BUGGY

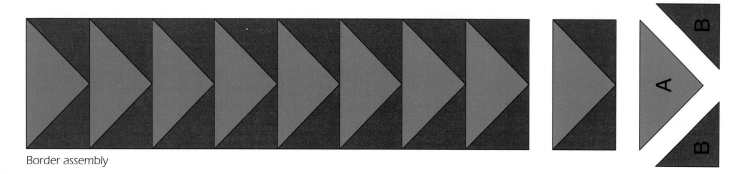

Border assembly

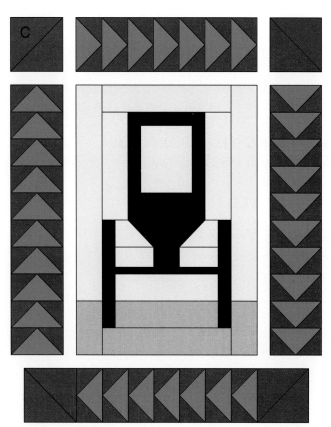

Quilt top assembly

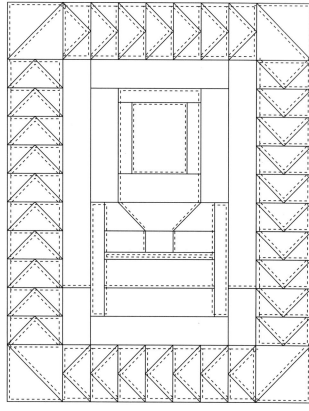

Quilting design

Patterns for SINGLE BUGGY

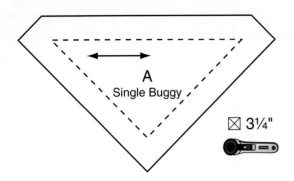

A
Single Buggy

⊠ 3¼"

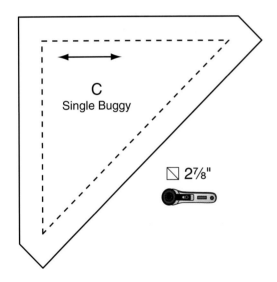

C
Single Buggy

◩ 2⅞"

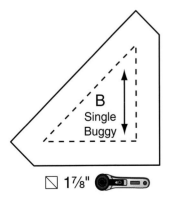

B
Single
Buggy

◩ 1⅞"

SINGLE BUGGY (with black border), 11" x 14"

Foundation Piecing Guides for SINGLE BUGGY

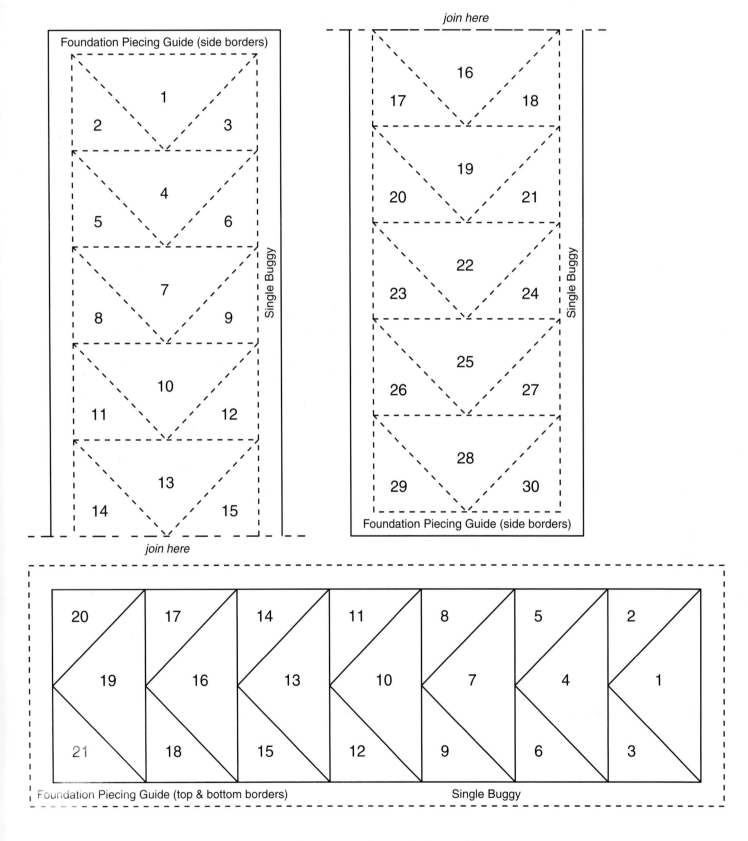

Foundation Piecing Guide (side borders)

1
2   3
4
5   6
7
8   9
10
11   12
13
14   15

Single Buggy

join here

join here

16
17   18
19
20   21
22
23   24
25
26   27
28
29   30

Single Buggy

Foundation Piecing Guide (side borders)

20   17   14   11   8   5   2
19   16   13   10   7   4   1
21   18   15   12   9   6   3

Foundation Piecing Guide (top & bottom borders)   Single Buggy

AT THE BARN RAISING

28" x 28"

This quilt is a variation of the Barn Raising pattern. The wood-grained fabrics represent the barn beams with the blue sky seen through the rafters. Buggies are quilted along the outer border to show how the Amish gather around to help with a barn raising.

CHOOSING FABRICS

A traditional look can be achieved in this quilt by using solid fabrics; however, printed fabrics can add a touch of personality. The use of solid fabric for the border is a good choice if you prefer a visible quilting design.

FABRIC REQUIREMENTS

For those patches that can be rotary cut, dimensions are given with the patterns. A lowercase "r" indicates that a patch should be reversed.

Fabric	Yards	Cutting Guide
Light brown	⅛	64 A
Med. brown	¼	32 A, 112 B
Dark brown	⅝	4 A, 32 C, 36 E, 12 F, 12 Fr
borders		2 strips 3½" x 22½"
		2 strips 3½" x 28½"
Blue	⅜	32 C, 1 D, 36 E, 12 F, 12 Fr
borders		2 strips 1¾" x 20"
		2 strips 1¾" x 22½"
Black	⅛	
borders		2 strips 1¼" x 18½"
		2 strips 1¼" x 20"
Brown binding	¼	4 strips 1¼" x 30"
Backing	1	
Batting		32" x 32"

 If you are using fabric with a directional pattern-like wood grain, align the template with the pattern rather than the grain line.

QUILT ASSEMBLY

Assemble the units in the following order:

Patches	Unit Assembly
Sew dark brown C patches to blue C patches.	Make 8
Join the CC units.	Make 4
Sew blue E patches to dark brown E patches.	Make 36
Sew dark brown C patches to blue F patches.	Make 12
Sew dark brown C patches to blue Fr patches.	Make 12
Join only four of the CF and CFr units.	Make 4
Sew blue C patches to dark brown F patches.	Make 12
Sew blue C patches to dark brown Fr patches.	Make 12
Join only eight of the CFr and CF units.	Make 8

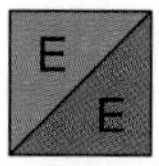

Using the assembled units, piece the following rows:

Row	Assembly

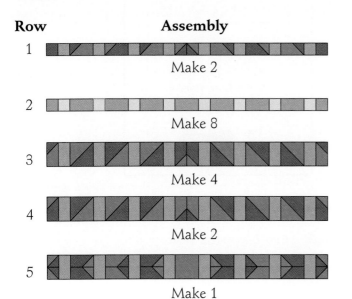

1
Make 2

2
Make 8

3
Make 4

4
Make 2

5
Make 1

Once each row is pieced, sew the rows together, matching seams.

Refer to the quilt top assembly diagram below to add the borders. Square up the quilt top and add the borders to the sides of the quilt first, then to the top and bottom. Square up the quilt again and join the remaining borders in the same order.

FINISHING YOUR QUILT

Layer the backing, batting, and quilt top, and baste together. Quilt as desired, or refer to the quilting design, page 36. Trim the quilt and add binding. Sew a casing to the back and sign your quilt as a finishing touch.

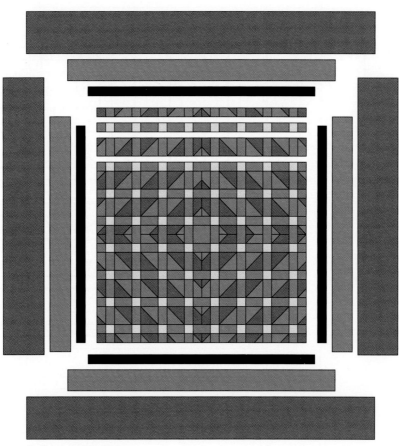

Quilt top assembly

Patterns for AT THE BARN RAISING

A
At the Barn
Raising

1¼"

At the Barn Raising

C

☒ 1⅝"

D
At the Barn Raising

2"

B
At the Barn Raising

2" x 1¼"

Quilting patterns on pages 55-61

E
At the Barn
Raising

☒ 2⅜"

F & Fr
At the Barn
Raising

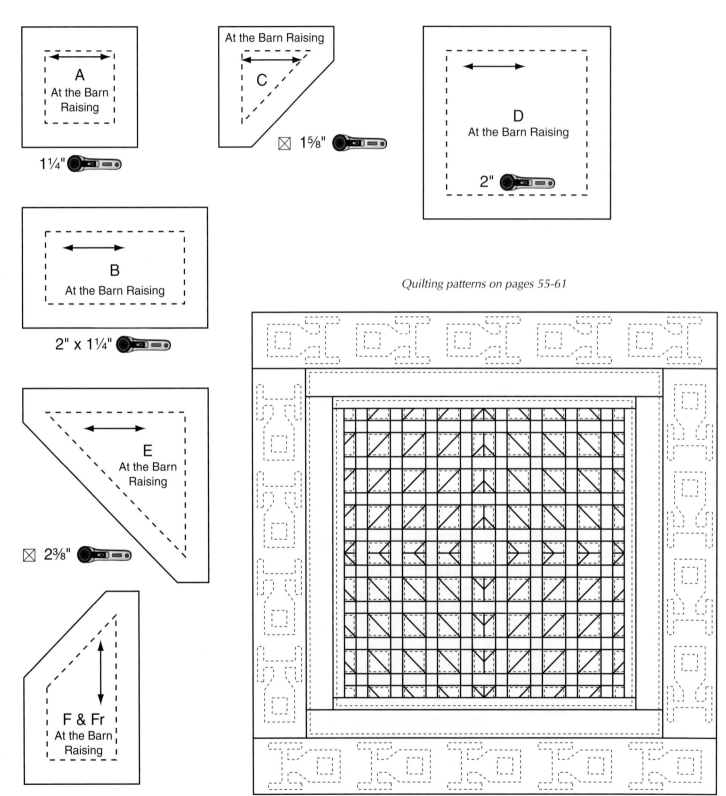

Quilting design

IRISH CHAIN

29" x 35½"

The beauty of this quilt is the dramatic presentation of blue fabric against black. The skill level of this pattern is deceiving because the piecing is much easier than it appears. Give it a try!

By changing the color arrangement, Irish Chain becomes a traditional Nine-Patch pattern, set on-point. The use of plaid fabrics gives this quilt a more modern look.

FABRIC REQUIREMENTS

IRISH CHAIN

For those patches that can be rotary cut, dimensions are given with the patterns.

Fabric	Yards	Cutting Guide
Blue	⅝	60 A
borders		2 strips 2" x 22½"
		2 strips 2" x 26"
Black	1⅜	48 A
		10 B, 6 C, 4 D
borders		2 strips 4" x 29"
		2 strips 4" x 29½"
Binding		4 strips 1½" x 36½"
Backing	1	
Batting		33" x 39½"

PLAID NINE-PATCH, page 39

12 plaids	fat eighths	5 A of each color
binding		2 strips 2" x 8" of each color
(piece to make 2 strips 2" x 31½" and 2 strips 2" x 38")		
Light gray	¼	6 C
Dark gray	¼	10 B, 4 D
White	¾	48 A
borders		2 strips 4" x 29"
		2 strips 4" x 29½"
Black	¼	
borders		2 strips 2" x 22½"
		2 strips 2" x 26"
Backing	1	
Batting		33" x 39½"

CHOOSING FABRICS FOR PLAID NINE-PATCH

Look for plaid fabrics that have grays, blacks, and greens. A marbled white or a white-on-white fabric will make the plaids stand out. It is helpful to purchase both gray fabrics at the same time to ensure they complement each other.

BLOCK CONSTRUCTION

Block trim size: 5". Refer to the block assembly diagram and make 12 Nine-Patch blocks.

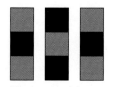

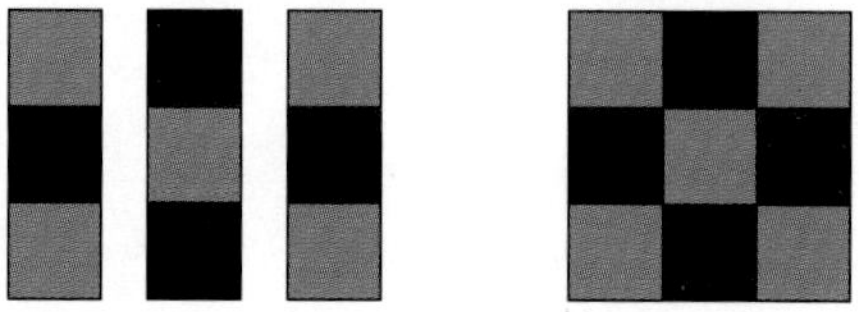

Block assembly

ASSEMBLING THE QUILT TOP

Refer to the quilt top assembly diagram, page 39, and arrange the Nine-Patches, corner triangles, side triangles, and center blocks. Sew the pieces together in diagonal rows as shown.

 Press the seam allowances in opposite directions on each row to avoid sewing over a double thickness of fabric.

Trim as necessary to square up the quilt top and add the borders to the sides of the quilt first, then to the top and bottom. Square up the quilt again and join the remaining borders in the same order.

FINISHING YOUR QUILT

Layer the backing, batting, and quilt top, and baste together. Quilt as desired or refer to the quilting designs, page 39. Trim your quilt and add binding. Sew a casing to the back and sign your quilt as a finishing touch.

Diagrams for IRISH CHAIN/PLAID NINE-PATCH

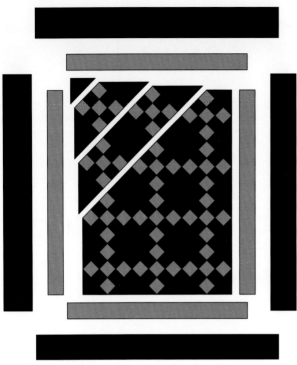

Quilt top assembly

PLAID NINE-PATCH, 29" x 35½"

Quilting patterns on pages 55–61

3" Cable Border, Quilting Stencil #101, Borders Made Easy by Quilting Made Easy, Inc. Coeur d'Alene, ID

Irish Chain quilting design

Plaid Nine-Patch quilting design

Patterns for IRISH CHAIN/PLAID NINE-PATCH

C
Irish Chain/Plaid Nine-Patch

5"

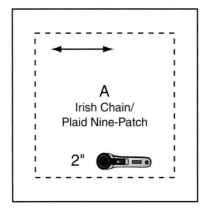

A
Irish Chain/
Plaid Nine-Patch

2"

Patterns for IRISH CHAIN/PLAID NINE-PATCH

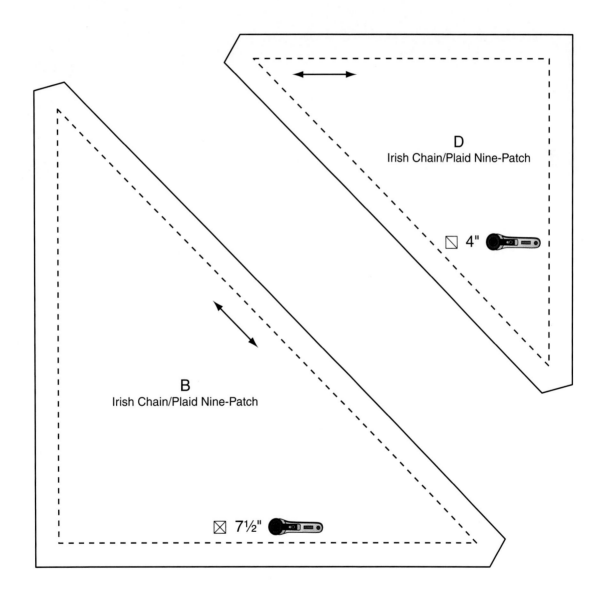

D
Irish Chain/Plaid Nine-Patch

◻ 4"

B
Irish Chain/Plaid Nine-Patch

⊠ 7½"

BARS

24" x 24"

This is a quick quilt to piece. The solid-color fabrics provide a perfect canvas for creative quilting. Feather stitching and crosshatch quilting were very typical on traditional bar quilts.

You can transform this traditional quilt into a beautiful batik showcase by using a variety of colorful fabrics.

FABRIC REQUIREMENTS

BARS

For those patches that can be rotary cut, dimensions are given with the patterns.

Fabric	Yards	Cutting Guide
Mauve	⅜	6 strips 3½" x 18½"
Blue	⅛	2 strips 3½" x 18½"
Pale blue	⅜	2 strips 3½" x 18½"
		4 squares 3½"
binding		4 strips 1¼" x 25"
Backing	⅞	
Batting		28" x 28"

BATIK BARS, page 44

Navy batik	¼	4 strips 3½" x 18½"
Lt. purple batik	⅛	4 squares 3½"
		1 strip 3½" x 18½"
5 assort. batiks	⅛ each	1 strip 3½" x 18½" of each color
Binding	¼	4 strips 1¼" x 25"
Backing	⅞	
Batting		28" x 28"

CHOOSING FABRICS FOR BATIK BARS

Batiks are great to work with because of the wonderful blends of color. Purple is the main color in this quilt. Choose colors that blend well with your dominant color choice. Lay out your fabrics to see if the combination of colors is pleasing before beginning.

ASSEMBLING THE QUILT TOP

Refer to the diagram to assemble the quilt top. Press the seam allowances on the middle and border strips in the same direction to make piecing the top and bottom borders smooth.

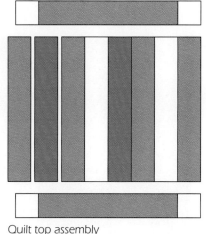

Quilt top assembly

 Marking the quilting lines with masking tape helps make straight lines that are easy to quilt. However, do not leave the tape on for more than a day because it may leave a sticky residue.

FINISHING YOUR QUILT

Layer the backing, batting, and quilt top, and baste together. Quilt as desired, or refer to the quilting designs, page 44. Trim your quilt and add binding. Sew a casing to the back, and sign your quilt as a finishing touch.

Diagrams for Bars/Batik Bars

Quilting patterns on pages 55–61

2" Feather Border with Corner, Quilting Stencil #528,
Quilting Creations International • Zoar, OH

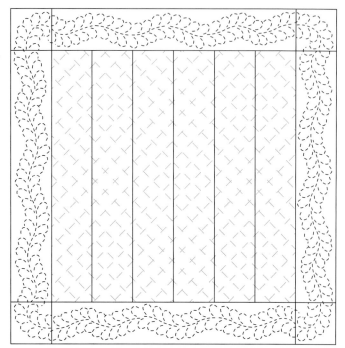

Bars quilting design

Batik Bars, 24" x 24"

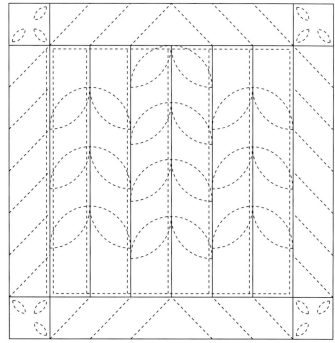

Batik Bars quilting design

SHOOFLY

33½ " x 41"

The slate gray fabric used in this quilt gives it an antique look. The red fabric adds a brilliant flash of color. The buggy wheels quilted in the center blocks add to the uniqueness of this quilt.

The change of colors to pastel in SHOOFLY LULLABY, page 47, makes it ideal for a baby.

FABRIC REQUIREMENTS
SHOOFLY

For those patches that can be rotary cut, dimensions are given with the patterns.

Fabric	Yards	Cutting Guide
Red	⅝	48 A, 48 B
binding		4 strips 1½" x 43"
Black	⅝	48 A, 12 B
borders		2 strips 2" x 26"
		2 strips 2" x 30½"
Gray	1¼	6 C, 10 D, 4 E
borders		2 strips 4½" x 34½"
		2 strips 4½" x 33½"
Backing	1⅜	
Batting		37½" x 45"

SHOOFLY LULLABY, page 47

12 pastels	fat eighths	4 A and 4 B of each fabric
White	1⅞	48 A, 12 B, 6 C, 10 D, 4 E
borders		2 strips 4½" x 33½"
		2 strips 4½" x 34½"
Yellow	¼	
borders		2 strips 2" x 30½"
		2 strips 2" x 26"
Purple	¼	
binding		4 strips 1½" x 43"
Backing	1¼	
Batting		37½" x 45"

CHOOSING FABRICS FOR SHOOFLY LULLABY

Pastels that have small white prints add to the softness of this color combination. This quilt contains 12 different pastels. The background fabric is a white-on-white print.

BLOCK CONSTRUCTION

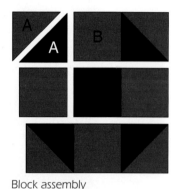

Block assembly

Block trim size: 5¾". Refer to the block assembly diagram and make 12 Shoofly blocks.

ASSEMBLING THE QUILT TOP

Refer to the quilt top assembly diagram, page 47, and arrange the Shoofly blocks, corner triangles, side triangles, and center blocks. Sew the pieces together in diagonal rows as shown.

 Press the seam allowances in opposite directions on each row to avoid sewing over a double thickness of fabric.

Trim as necessary to square up the quilt top. Add the borders to the sides of the quilt first, then to the top and bottom. Square up the quilt again and join the remaining borders in the same order.

FINISHING YOUR QUILT

Layer the backing, batting, and quilt top, and baste together. Quilt as desired, or refer to the quilting designs, page 47. The pattern for Shoofly Lullaby is very easy to machine quilt. Trim your quilt and add binding. Sew a casing to the back for wallhangings, and sign your quilt as a finishing touch.

Diagrams for SHOOFLY/SHOOFLY LULLABY

Quilt top assembly

SHOOFLY LULLABY, 33½" x 41"

Shoofly quilting design

Quilting patterns on pages 55-61

Shoofly Lullaby quilting design

Patterns for SHOOFLY/SHOOFLY LULLABY

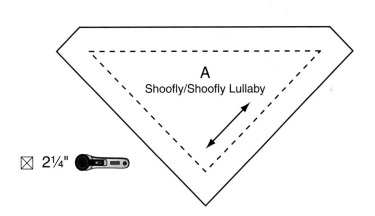

A
Shoofly/Shoofly Lullaby

⊠ 2¼"

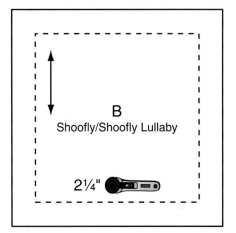

B
Shoofly/Shoofly Lullaby

2¼"

C
Shoofly/Shoofly Lullaby

5¾"

Patterns for SHOOFLY/SHOOFLY LULLABY

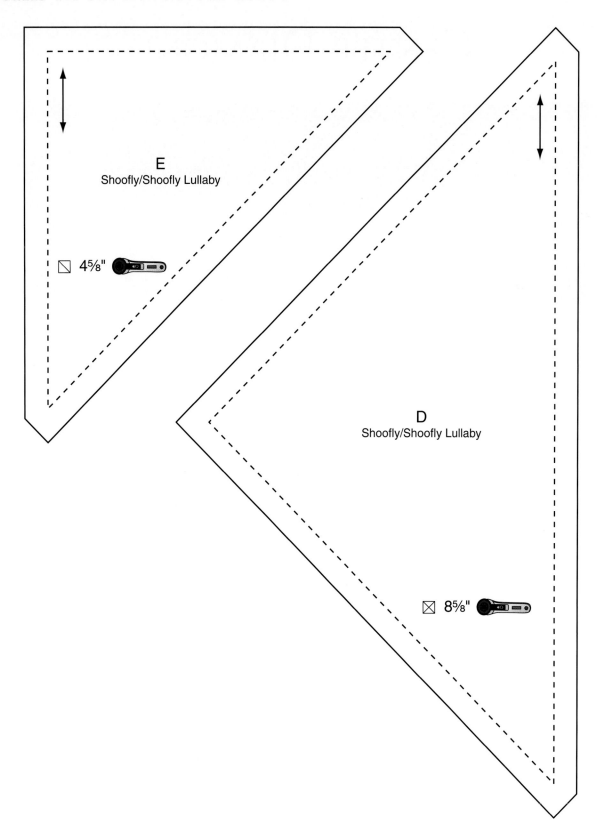

E
Shoofly/Shoofly Lullaby

◻ 4⅝"

D
Shoofly/Shoofly Lullaby

⊠ 8⅝"

CENTER DIAMOND

24" x 24"

This traditional pattern is simple in its design and is an easy quilt to piece. Part of the beauty lies in the intricate quilting that the large pieces allow.

Printed fabrics give this traditional pattern a new look. The name for PEACOCK DIAMOND, as well as the quilting designs, were inspired by the lovely peacock feathers in one of the fabrics.

FABRIC REQUIREMENTS
CENTER DIAMOND
For those patches that can be rotary cut, dimensions are given with the patterns.

Fabric	Yards	Cutting Guide
Red	¼	4 A, 4 C, 1 D
Blue	⅛	4 B
Light green	¼	2 (E) squares 8⅞" cut once diagonally
Dark green borders	⅜	4 (F) strips 4½" x 16½"
Med. green binding	¼	4 strips 1¼" x 26½"
Backing	¾	
Batting		28" x 28"

PEACOCK DIAMOND, page 52

Teal	¼	1 D
Light purple	⅛	4 B
Dark purple borders	⅜	4 (F) strips 4½" x 16½"
Teal-purple	¼	2 (E) squares 8⅞" cut once diagonally
Black binding	¼	4 A, 4 C 4 strips 1¼" x 26"
Backing	¾	
Batting		28" x 28"

ASSEMBLING THE QUILT TOP
Refer to the quilt top assembly diagram below to assemble the quilt top.

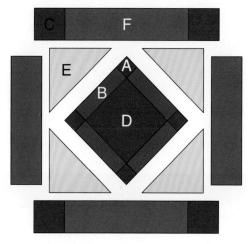

Quilt top assembly

FINISHING YOUR QUILT
Layer the backing, batting, and quilt top, and baste together. Quilt as desired, or refer to the quilting designs, page 52. Trim your quilt and add binding. Add a casing to the back, and sign your quilt as a finishing touch.

 Add sparkle to your quilting with gold metallic thread. Using short lengths of thread helps keep it from breaking or tangling.

Diagrams for Center Diamond/Peacock Diamond

Quilting patterns on pages 55–61

3½" Feathered Circle, Quilting Stencil #405,
4" Pumpkin Seed Border, Quilting Stencil #582,
Quilting Creations International • Zoar, OH

Center Diamond quilting design

Peacock Diamond, 24" x 24"

Peacock Diamond quilting design

Patterns for CENTER DIAMOND/PEACOCK DIAMOND

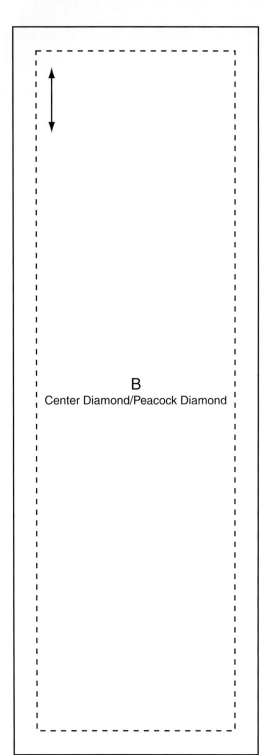

B
Center Diamond/Peacock Diamond

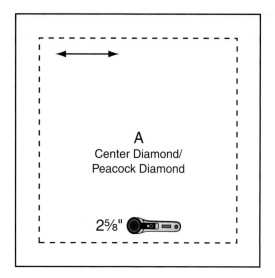

A
Center Diamond/
Peacock Diamond

2⅝"

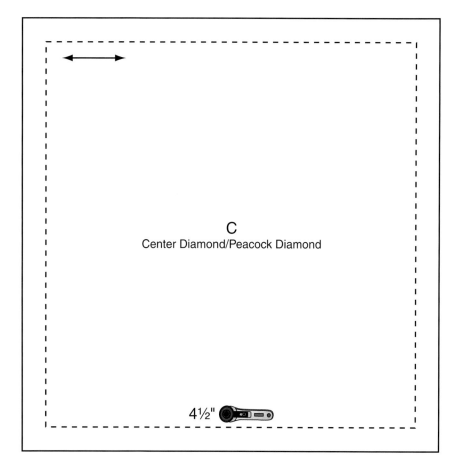

C
Center Diamond/Peacock Diamond

4½"

Patterns for CENTER DIAMOND/PEACOCK DIAMOND

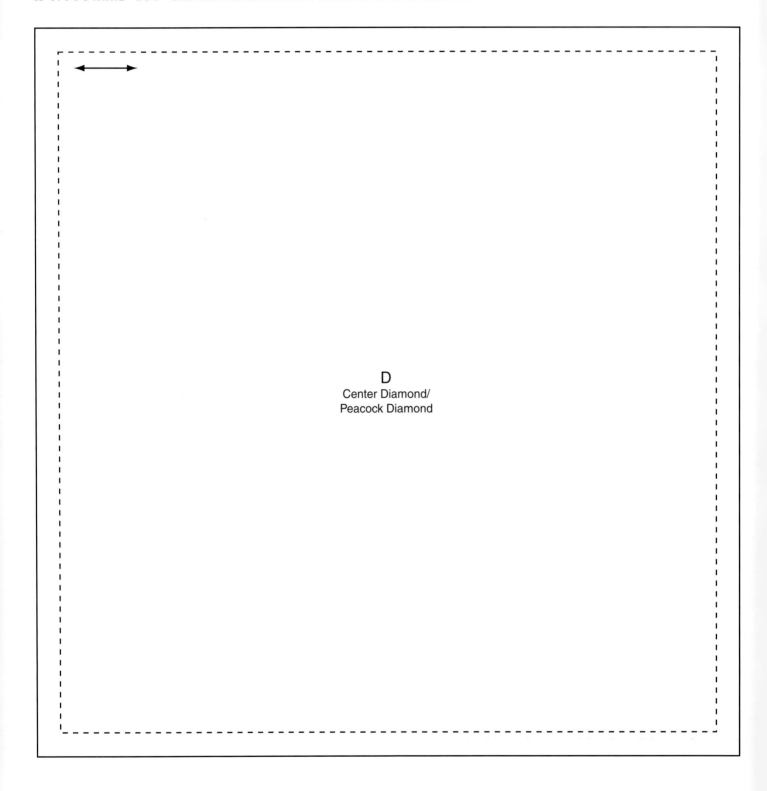

D
Center Diamond/
Peacock Diamond

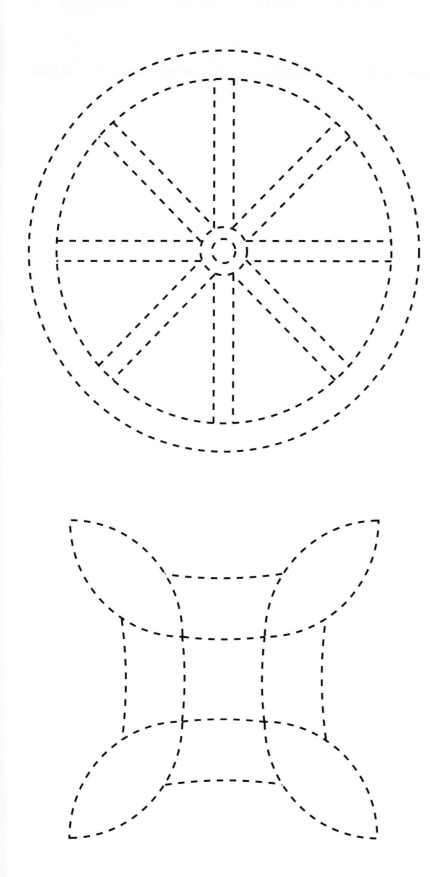

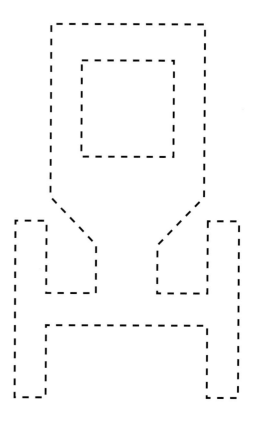

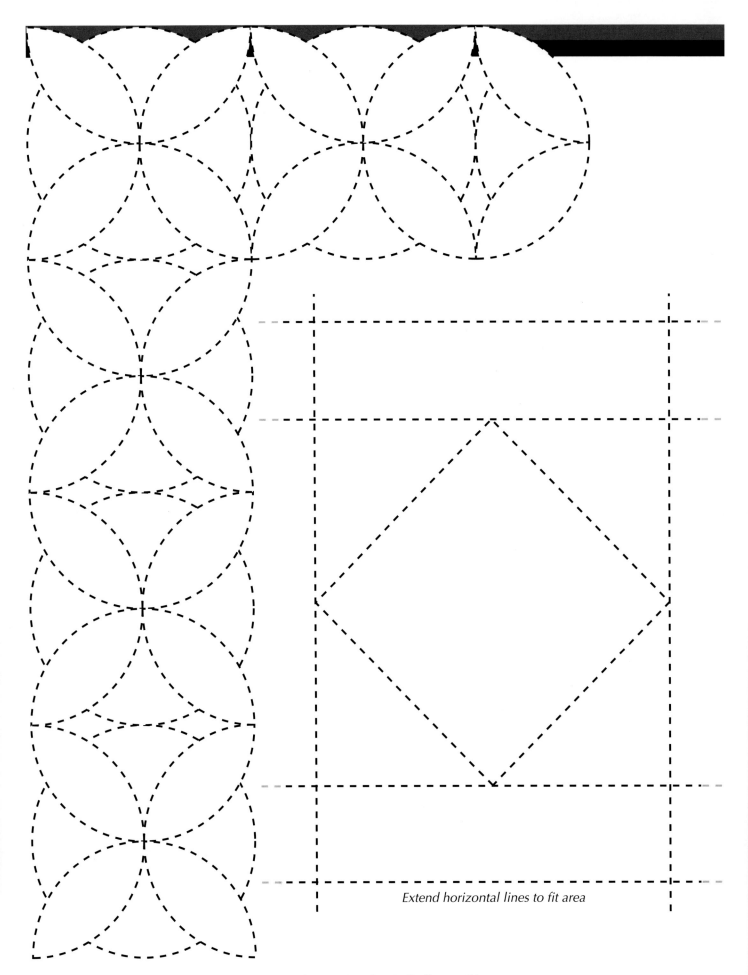

Extend horizontal lines to fit area

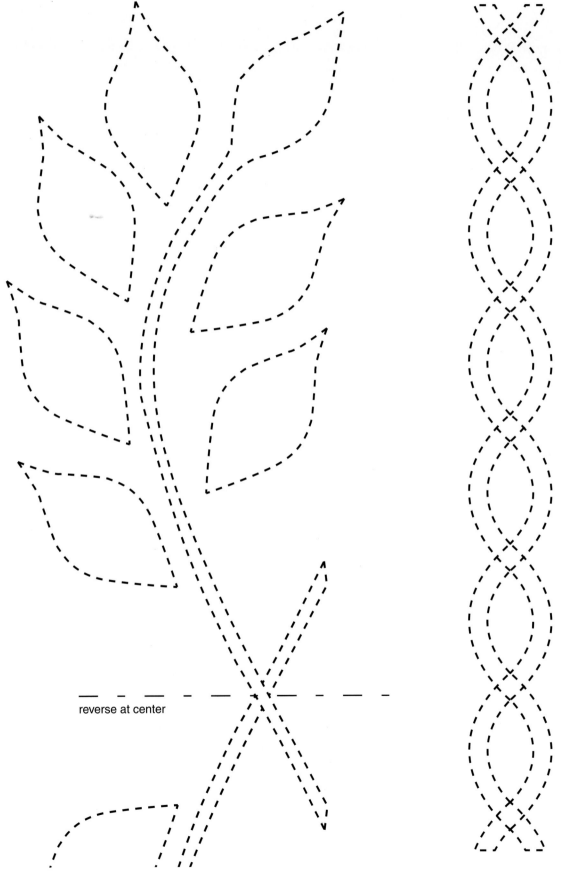

reverse at center

BIBLIOGRAPHY

Bishop, Robert and Elizabeth Safanda. *A Gallery of Amish Quilts*.
New York: E.P. Dutton, Inc., 1976.

Pellman, Rachel and Kenneth. *A Treasury of Amish Quilts*.
Intercourse, PA: Good Books, 1990.

Pellman, Rachel and Kenneth. *The World of Amish Quilts*.
Intercourse, PA: Good Books, 1984.

Pottinger, David. *Quilts from the Indiana Amish: A Regional Collection*.
New York: E.P. Dutton, Inc., 1983.

Scott, Stephen. *Plain Buggies: Amish, Mennonite, and Brethren Horse Drawn Transportation*.
Intercourse, PA: Good Books, 1998.

Yoder, Doyle and Leslie A. Kelly. *America's Amish Country*.
Berlin, OH: America's Amish Country Publications, 1992

OTHER AQS BOOKS

This is only a small selection of the books available from the American Quilter's Society. AQS books are known worldwide for timely topics, clear writing, beautiful color photos, and accurate illustrations and patterns. The following books are available from your local bookseller, quilt shop, or the public library.

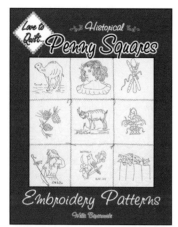

#4753   US $12.95

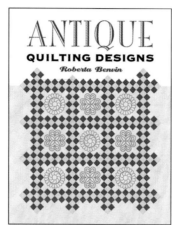

#5849   US $21.95

#5708   US $22.95

#5705   US $22.95

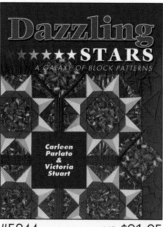

#5844   US $21.95

#5756   US $19.95

#5013   US $14.95

#5764   US $19.95

#5853   US $18.95

Look for these books nationally or call 1-800-626-5420